YIELD

---

*"Just when I think I have learned the way to live,
life changes."*

-Hugh Prather

YIELD

Your Dreams, Your Love, Your Life

Quintin C. Lindblad

Pictures & Postcards Publishing
Copyright 2015

Self-published as Pictures & Postcards Publishing.

First Printing: September 2015

ISBN: 978-1515272410

Dedication:

To Papa & Nana Hansen:

For living a life that was completely yielded to your Savior and showing me what it looks like to approach marriage as a full-blown partnership. I pray Erin and I can run our race as beautifully as you did – together!

To Erin:

For trusting me, loving me and, most importantly, believing in me like no one else ever could. I love you!

Find more copies of Yield at Amazon.com.

Foreword

You cannot move forward if you are unwilling to reflect on where you've been. We shouldn't live in the past but we need to spend some time there so we know what needs to change in our future. Lately, introspection and self-evaluation are being underrated. We're more encouraged to simply be true to ourselves and do what feels right than we are to evaluate whether or not those things are godly and right. That idea mirrors the fact that few people at or near age 30 feel the need to look back. After all, what is 30 years? For most, 30 years is a life that is just getting started. But Quint has decided to look back and evaluate.

I remember Quint from high school and the years after and his many jobs and goals. I wondered when he was going to pick a career, a hobby, something, (anything!) and stick with it. This book is a perfect response to that question. His answer is that we make our plans and dream our dreams but unless we are wholly yielded to God they will be just that - plans and dreams, not reality. God is the one who brings things to fruition. God is the one who does more in us and through us than we can even imagine. We must simply yield. And this is not to say that it's wrong to plan and dream. But I wonder how many of us dream about what God would have us do as opposed to how much of that dreaming is all about us?

This book encourages the reader to stop and take a look at the life they're living. Is this the life you want? Is this a life that is 100% yielded to God? When life isn't going the way we want, we tend to look for any reason why other than our own choices. Yield suggests that it is the choice to humbly submit to God that puts life into the right perspective. I wish there had been a book like this for me coming out of high school. I would have read it and then given copies away to every graduating class of seniors that came through my youth ministry. Quint looks back and writes for the 19 or 20 year old looking forward and helps them pave the way for success, not necessarily in finance or business, but in life. A life yielded to God. If I can look back at my 30's and learn as much from them as Quint has from his 20's I will be blessed indeed.

-Chris Vitarelli, August 2015

Preface

This book is meant to serve as a *practical reflection*. As I look back on the last 10 years of my life – in the ever-changing landscape known as "adulthood" – certain themes keep popping up and feeling so blatant. But then I realize it is not that these themes are just blatant or obvious. It is that they are TRUE. *And truth always stands!* So in an attempt to capture just *some* of the principles that helped me survive my 20's, I offer to you *YIELD...*

Contents:

YIELD

How We Got Here

YIELD

"It is hard to make good decisions when you are holding a chainsaw above your head." That is how I'd always planned to start my first book. It stems from the time I held my large and powerful chainsaw ABOVE MY HEAD and proceeded to cut a tree limb that I needed to remove. I thought to myself, "I'll know when to move out of the way." That was easily a Top Ten dumb decision for me. I'm very grateful I avoided getting killed by the massive portion of tree that came dropping out of the sky and was then smart enough to call it a day for Quint the Lumberjack. So now you know a little bit more about me and I have succeeded in using what I hope was an epic opening sentence to a book. Let us proceed!

I have tried to write before. I had a failed attempt at a blog once. Before that I started a book on my old college laptop. I was more concerned with how big my book should be and what size would look best on a shelf. (I wanted it to feel just right in your hands but also be thick enough that you knew I had a lot to offer). Obviously, that died quickly and I don't know that I even saved the file.

I've never even really done a great job journaling. I have tried to start that habit but it just never felt right. I would get done and think to myself "Why would I ever want to read this and re-live this day?" It's not that my days were particularly awful. I am just a "windshield" kind of guy, not a "rear-view mirror" kind of guy. I have a pretty rock solid memory, so I figured if something was that important I would be able to recall it without having to keep a journal.

In spite of all that here I sit, typing out what I hope to be a finished work someday - soon. Not another failed attempt, not another start without a finish. But honestly, I know that this time is different. This time I have a message that I want to convey. These chapters and principles are drawn from experiences that have stood true for the first ten years of my adult life and I want to share them with you. My hope is that anyone who reads this book will see some of his or her own story shine through. This project certainly isn't intended to tell "my story." My goal in taking on this task is to point to eight different places in Scripture that might illuminate Christ's plan and purpose for your life. Eight unique principles that can absolutely stand-alone and help you - but can also be united to reveal a place of great stability and peace. Each chapter will begin with the Scripture that the entire principle is based on. Ok, let's do this!

YOUR PLANS

YIELD

Proverbs 16:9 – In their hearts humans plan their course, but the LORD establishes their steps.

There are a TON of self-help books out there today. The western world has made quite a to-do over success, growth, goals and achievement. It seems to be a never-ending process of learn and strive, learn and strive. As beautiful as it is to know that if we set our minds to something it can be achieved, I have to wonder, "are we missing something?"

When God created Adam and Eve, one of the first things he gave them was a job (Genesis 1:28)[1], so there is no doubt at all that work is very important. We teach our children to work. We seek gainful employment for ourselves. But at the end of the day, if all we have done is set a goal to acquire a job, complete tasks and earn some money, are we really fulfilling the roles we were created for?

YIELD

I have had no less than 30 jobs in my life (inspiring, I know). My first job was a cashier at a grocery store at the age of 16. Pretty typical first job, I think. My least enjoyable job was the spring that I did blow-in insulation in attics and crawl spaces. And probably my most exciting venture was the winter that I went "dumpster-diving" for flight vouchers and in turn sold airline tickets online for straight cash. There was no overhead to my "business" unless you count the clothes that I probably should have burned after a night of digging through the local fast food restaurant's dumpster! (My parents declared, "we are Lindblad's, we don't dig through dumpsters." When they saw the equivalent of three round-trip tickets and one sale for $250.00 after the first night, they quickly were on board with my miniature business. My mom even bought one from me.) The constant that I have seen through all of these crazy and varying experiences is this: *most people are just trying to make "enough" money*. There is no shortage of demands in this life and we live in a society that seems to lessen the demands with an increase in funds. The more we can make, the less pressure we will most likely feel. This is the story, anyways.

Jesus had plenty to say about money during His ministry. The Bible is full of verses on how God would have us handle it. But I am certainly not any type of financial guru. I have several that I enjoy reading and listening to, but my goal with this first chapter is to attack something entirely different: your PLAN.

Plans are a very hyped up part of our world. We encourage our children to plan. We advise our high school age kids to pick good colleges so that when they get into said colleges they can pick their life plan before they have ever experienced real life. We are a "plan happy" society. And I actually used to subscribe strongly to the mindset "Plan your work and work your plan." But in recent years I have been forced to rethink this common saying and its value in my life. Allow me to explain:

Having a plan is vital; no it is PARAMOUNT, to seeing success in life. I believe God gives us the instruction to "train up a child in the way he should go[2]" because its important that as parents we don't just "wing it" and hope that our kids turn out okay. But I have also found that I needed to be careful my plans weren't always written out with a pen. I needed to start grabbing that No. 2 pencil and filling out my Day-Timer with it instead.

You see I am a fairly extreme person. And I know I am not the only one like this. When I really buy into something, others can get more than they asked for a lot of the time. Maybe you can relate.

YIELD

Early on in my adult life, I was what you would most likely call *immovable*. I heard the "plan your work" mantra and I went all in. If plans were what mattered, I was going to create the best one I possibly could – and then stick to it! But I learned that most times my best-laid plans fell far short of what God had actually intended for my life.

God knew you and me before the dawn of time. He saw what was coming long before we had breathed our first breath. So with that omniscient vision that only He possesses, He saw all of the twists and turns that would happen in our lives. I am in a very different place at 30 years old than I ever would have predicted. You could probably say the same about your life. But I look back and see God's grace all over every failure, trial, success and victory that I have encountered over the past ten years. I have had opportunities (and made attempts) to build businesses, buy businesses, buy houses, be a rock star, be a worship leader and many other things. And yet, here I sit, feeling the call to go into ministry full-time and seriously weighing some great opportunities that lie before me – like writing this book and working on a new worship record. Neither of which were anywhere near my personal plans over the past ten years.

Had any of my plans worked out, I would not be at the "fork in the road" that I stand at today. God has actually completely flipped my life upside down and brought me to this new place just over the last eighteen months. And yet, without all of the aforementioned events, I would not be who I am or feel at all ready for a life spent serving God and His people full-time!

What I have learned, and the principle that LEAPS off the page at me from Proverbs 16:9 is this: we are all full of ideas, hopes, dreams, prejudices and agendas. No matter how near to God we draw ourselves, we will always have some natural tendencies to lean *our way* and do *our thing.* But in the end, He is placing our steps right where He wants them. We can certainly do things to delay God's Will for our lives but if we are striving to please Him, seek Him and do what is right in His eyes then He will see to it that we land in all the right places that He has for us. It's who He is and it's what He does!

Fortunately for me, God is very gracious and He has regularly surrounded me with people who are equally as gracious. When I have showed my obstinate, immovable side that wants to cling to the plan I have drawn out, He has lovingly showed me it will be all right to just relax and trust Him. (Not all of these instances have been as calm and serene as that sentence makes them sound, but the lesson is the same!) What I have learned through all of these circumstances is that plans are great, but when we are called into Christ's flock and He is our shepherd we have to be willing to follow where He leads and not force things to go our way. Even when it feels like a wide, empty space of questions and confusion, He is doing His work – in our lives and in the lives of those around us!

So I want to close this first chapter by posing some questions: when did life shift to a universal plan of "get a good job?" Or "just make some good money?" Where is the fulfillment found in just going through motions for an amount of money that we deem "enough?" I have always wanted to *live a purpose.* That being said, there were times in my life where I NEEDED to just go make some cash and alleviate the pressure (a la dumpster diving gig). And I'm sure there will be times like that in your life - if there haven't been already. But at the end of our lives, the true joy and legacy that we will leave will fall upon the shoulders of our *purpose.* Who have we helped? What have we done? What did we stand for? The plans may change but let's trust Him for clearly directed steps that fulfill His mission and lead us into His reality!

Questions:

1) How can we build lives that have gainful employment and also unite that with a purpose that is fulfilling?

2) In what ways can we build our own plans but also allow for the Lord to intervene with His will?

3) Can we sabotage His will for our lives with our own plans?

HIS REALITY

YIELD

Proverbs 19:21 - *Many are the plans in a person's heart, but it is the LORD's purpose that prevails.*

If my plans from age 20 had worked out, I would be a full-time Rock and Roll musician. And if my plans from age 23 had worked out, I would be an entrepreneur with a very flexible schedule. If my plans from age 26 had worked out, I would be in a full-time business partnership. By 28, I was kind of over making plans. And here is the ironic part: you could easily read that and think that I have been a flighty guy who couldn't or still can't make up his mind. Nothing could be further from the truth. I was very resolute in each of those phases of my 20's. I found it hard to find people equally as resolute sometimes but that didn't bother me. I truly wanted all of those things to come to fruition and would go it alone if that's what it took. But for whatever reason, each time I dug in my heels, I just couldn't get traction. I felt like I was running each of those races with something missing. They all made logical sense (well maybe not the Rock and Roll part, but it made lots of emotional sense…and I was only 20). They all made financial sense. They all appealed to a part of me that felt good and alive when I was in the middle of them. Now that I can look back and do some investigating, I think I have found what was missing.

Despite all of my best efforts and hopes and attempts to make the aforementioned plans Godly, they lacked His purpose. He has used them to absolutely *serve a purpose* and prepare me for what is to come. But they weren't His ultimate purpose for my life. God knew when He made you and He knew when He made me just what role would best help advance His kingdom. And He designed us all so that there is a role that only we can play! I realize now that He used all of the things that I came up with in my 20's to bring me to a place of understanding. A place of wisdom. A place of compassion. And not all of those events were of my doing. I believe He brought me through many of those opportunities to make me more like Him. The hard part during some of those times was realizing it and letting Him make me more like Himself!

How often do we miss out on His role for our lives because we just tune out? Because we are so dead set on bringing our plans to fruition? Is it possible that at times we desire His will a little less than we desire our own?   Like I shared in Chapter 1, I have learned to be very careful not to get so dug in to my plans that I find myself saying "No" to His will. In Proverbs 18:16 we read "A man's gift makes room for Him, and brings him before great men." Are we allowing that to be true in our lives? I read that and feel a whole load of pressure come off. Why would we need to strive so greatly to *achieve our desires* when His Word tells us that by operating in our gifts, we will find promotion? Allow me to translate: by seeking to serve our God in Heaven, with the gifts that He has blessed us with, we will find ourselves in situations we could never have imagined or orchestrated on our own!   What could be better? Here's a personal story:

I have played music since I was 5 years old. I started with piano lessons and excelled quite a bit with that. Then I picked up a guitar – and I was at home! I taught myself to play guitar starting around age 14. All of the training I had on piano just flowed over to this new instrument and I was in love. When I was 17, I did what every 17 year old that plays 2 instruments and sings should do: I started a Punk Rock band. And we were pretty good (which is about as good as you need to be when playing punk rock). Over the next 3 years we played around 50 shows, recorded a 7 song CD and sold or gave away about 200 copies. All in all, a successful venture for a bunch of teens that just wanted to have fun and make noise.

When we broke up the band because it was time for each of us to chase our respective girlfriends all over the country, I came to a new place in my walk with Christ and I realized something that ended up changing my life. I had been playing music for me. Even when it wasn't for my band, but I was invited to play at different churches, I was only saying yes because I enjoyed it. Not to worship or praise God. So I made a very difficult but surprisingly mature choice. I told God that I would lay down music until I was able to do it for Him and Him alone. I knew myself very well and that meant if I got involved again too soon, I would be back in the same spot. So I waited. I figured it would be a few months or maybe even a year before I was back doing what I love, but in a more pure capacity. Eight years later, I still wasn't playing music - anywhere!

I was attending a church about 45 minutes from where I lived. Their band was awesome and their services were dynamite. My wife, Erin and I were happy just not very involved. Then I got a text for lunch from an old friend who was the pastor of a newer church right in my hometown.

Honestly, I knew very little about the church but I knew they were doing their best to reach people for Christ in a new and relevant way. The first thing he mentioned when we sat down was that they were in need of a new Worship Director. He had never heard me play. He knew I was in love with my church at a distance. He wasn't even asking if I would consider it, he was really just informing me how their church plant was going – and yet I knew that Proverbs 18:16 was happening in my life as we sat over a Buffalo Chicken Salad and a Pulled Pork Sandwich. After 8 years of giving music back to Jesus and waiting on HIM to place me back on a stage, the time had come.

For the next 60 minutes I asked all sorts of details from him because I wanted to be sure what I might be signing my family up for. At the end of our lunch I declared, "I think I could help you out." He was shocked, I was shocked and when I got home my wife, Erin was REALLY shocked! But that decision to wait on God and listen for when *He moved* is the reason we are involved in ministry today. That choice to *yield* to Him, but also remain patient and listen to Him brought us full circle to live a life we never could have imagined or planned for on our own.

When we read, "many are the plans in the mind of man" I think we all know exactly what is being referenced. Just yesterday I heard a sports radio host describe how he felt like he "had his golf game under control" and was also "ready to quit" in the same 4 hour round of golf! We humans tend to be pretty influenced by our experiences. We swing like a pendulum at times. One minute we are on top of the world because of how seamlessly we changed lanes on an unfamiliar highway and the next we have serious doubts about our intelligence, all because we made a wrong turn in a new city we have never even visited! It is kind of humorous and kind of sad, really. But God knows that about us. It was not His original design, but it is part of the aftermath of living in this fallen world. He created us and had great desires for a relationship and purpose with us before we were even on the scene. And so, in His infinite love, grace and wisdom, He prepared in advance to see His purpose fulfilled and to use us as His instruments to do it. He set Proverbs 19:21 into motion so that we might experience a fulfilled life.

You can be assured that He is working out the details in your life too! You might even have a similar story you could tell that shows His goodness and direction over a long period of time. Don't take it for granted! If you don't feel you have that story in your life yet, just rest in His vast provision. He wants to do the same for you! He will do the same for you! Know that His purpose has stood until now and will continue to stand in your life. Just let go and yield to Him!

Questions:

1)   Is it discouraging or freeing that no matter what we do, the Lord's purpose will stand?

2)   When we operate in our God-given gifts, what promises can we rest in?

3)   What is the most frustrating part about the "waiting on Him" stage? How about the most encouraging part?

IT'S OK!

YIELD

Psalm 73:26 – My flesh and my heart may fail, but God is the strength of my heart and my portion forever.

I wish I could tell you that I was just this calm, patient guy for those eight years of not doing music. But I definitely was not. I got discouraged. I was confused. I even became jealous of Justin Bieber! His movie Never Say Never came out and I was like "He is 14! If I had a break like that when I was 14 I could have been somebody." (Please don't stop reading my book just because I tell the whole story!) Honestly, I kind of just gave up on music after a while and thought to myself, "I will just play music for fun on my front porch or teach my kids someday or whatever." And I had grown Ok with that. But it definitely did hurt at times.

Somewhere along the way, this verse from Psalm 73 came into my life. Every time I read it, I still find myself encouraged like it is the first time. Because here is what I read: *Guess what! You will come up short. You will maybe even give up sometimes. But God will fill in your gaps. He is your strength when you have none. He'll take care of the details. Forever.*

I know, quite the paraphrase. I'm drawing some things out that aren't exactly front and center. But I think they are in there if we really dig!

There will be times when we have no natural reasons to hold out hope. We will give in before He has signed off on the situation. For me it was music, but what is it for you? What areas of your life make your heart come alive but it's just been "too long" or "too hard" and you think maybe it will never happen? Don't give up on God! He certainly hasn't given up on you.

Life is this crazy paradox. The Bible tells us that it is "but a vapor[1]" and at the same time, life is really long. It is no sprint that is for sure. I have known people who have had 3 or 4 *careers* in their lifetimes. Not jobs, careers. In fact there are crazy statistics now about my generation changing jobs up to 5 times before they are 30 years old[2]! We humans can do a lot of stuff over 60 plus years of adulthood. So it is imperative that we do not give up on a desire that God himself has placed in our hearts. As we draw near to Him, He will see to it that those Godly desires He has placed in our hearts do indeed come to pass AND He will work them out in ways that are more pleasing to Him than our best attempts could ever achieve on our own! Remember, "...a man's *gifts* make room for him." God gave you those gifts and He will also give you the platform to use those gifts for His glory and for Kingdom impact. But we must allow Him to do His work and make that happen. Remember, it is *Him directing our steps* and *His purpose that will stand*.

As I read through Psalm 73 last winter, I wrote a song from the study notes and the verses in the passage that deeply impacted me. The premise is this: so many times we see the gain of others and are discouraged. (Probably the second most-asked question after "why do bad things happen to good people?" is "why do good things happen for bad people.") In Psalm 73, we find the writer realizing that God's truth and plan will ultimately stand. He realizes that nothing is gained by turning to the ways of the wicked. Even in their prosperity, the end of the story is written; so do not lose heart in your troubles OR in their promotion! And do not let one magnify the other.

Your struggles are not worse because they are succeeding; nor are their successes better because you are in a struggle. At the end of this day and everyday, God is in control and God will be glorified. Lean in to Him, let Him do His work in you and let the story play out as He has predetermined. Become better through your struggle by letting Him perfect you. Nothing is a surprise to God the Father. He controls it all!

I certainly know that these words are pretty easy to type and can even be fairly easy to read, but the true test is believing them in the midst of the struggle. And while that certainly is not easy, through Him it is possible! We have all been in that spot where we feel like life is unfair or God has forgotten us. It is in verses like Psalm 73:26 that He is saying "I forgive your failure before it has even happened and I am still in control even when it doesn't feel like it. Trust me, love me, and love others. I will always be enough for you." It is true and it is good because He is true and He is good!

Take a moment to think on the fact that while you may come up short from time to time, you are loved and cared for by a God who has promised to be your strength *forever.* When that really soaks in, you will find a new kind of freedom and peace that surpasses anything you have ever known!

Questions:

1) Why do we tend to assume good things happening for bad people has anything to do with us?

2) How much encouragement can we draw from our God who says that no matter how often we fail, "He is our strength and portion forever?"

3) What Godly desires have you laid aside, thinking they will never materialize? Will you pick them up again?

YIELD

LET'S BACK UP

YIELD

***John 14:6** – Jesus answered, "I am the way and the truth and the life. No one comes to the Father except through me."*

I'm not going to lie. I am really excited about everything that I just typed! I mean it is like half of a book! That being said, I truly hope that this chapter isn't too late. I am banking on my captivating stories, witty humor and sloppy, "rookie" writing style to have kept you at least this long. Because the next few pages are by far the most important pages I will write!

Everything I have shared so far can be a truly great help in your life. I know that it has been for me the last ten years. Not because it is original or because I thought of a new thing that's never been written. It can be helpful because it is from God's Word and hopefully you are starting to see how this Book that is over 2,000 years old still really does apply in our lives today. It is timeless! But none of that matters if you haven't met Jesus and realized the role that He desires to play in your life.

In my many times leading worship I have played a countless number of closing songs at the end of some very powerful messages. And as people have been invited to come forward and pray with the pastor or just kneel at the altar and cry out to Jesus, I have seen some awesome things. Lives have been literally transformed as people have realized their need for a fresh start. But I have also observed many who fight it. Tears welling up in their eyes, emotions all over their faces, and yet they stay in their seats. My heart bursts with emotion for both sets of people and here is what I would love to do every time, regardless of their response: I would love to take off my guitar, walk up to the broken soul that stands before me and give them a hug. And then I want to share with them this revelation that changed my life:

Jesus loves you so much. We live in this broken and fallen world. So many bad things have happened before we ever arrived on the scene. We have done some of those bad things to people and some of them have been done to us. And it hurts.

And I'm sorry for all the guilt and shame and pain that have happened in your life. And so is Jesus. It breaks His heart too. In fact, He was so hurt by what hadn't even happened to you yet that He came to earth and paid an unthinkable price to get you back. Because He loves you and when He created you, He desired so many good things for your life. But this broken world has gotten in the way and tried to mess it up. Don't fight Him any longer. Don't feel guilty any longer. Just embrace who He is and what He has done for you. Accept it, meet Him right here and enter the relationship of a lifetime. Let Him fill your gaps. Let Him be your strength. Let Him heal your wounds. It won't happen overnight, but if you give Him the chance it will happen!

That's a pretty loaded paragraph, I know. But it's TRUE and that's what makes it good! *Jesus is your everything whether you know it or not.* I pray that if you have made it to this point in the book and have never heard that before, that you would take a minute and cry out to Jesus to save you, redeem you and start helping you heal. He is the Way, the Truth and the Life. It is by Him that you will enter Heaven and meet Father God someday. All the things I have shared or will share rest on the fact that you have made Jesus your Savior and are pursuing Him like the Treasure that He is. Jesus

YIELD

Christ was not just a "good man" or a Great Prophet. He was and is the living Son of God! He came to Earth as a man, showed us the Father with His life and paid the only price that would buy back God's fallen children. You are one of those fallen children, but He has redeemed you! Embrace His invitation of *new life!*

It sounds pretty simple, doesn't it? It actually can sound *too simple*. So let me be honest with you: IT IS SIMPLE BUT IT'S NOT ALWAYS EASY. And Jesus never said it would be easy. He warns of trials and tribulations but He also tells us in John 16:33 to "Take heart for I have overcome the world!" When all is spinning around us, we have an Anchor. I once heard a pastor say, "You don't choose Jesus so it will become easy, you choose Him so you can understand why it is hard." Life will be hard with or without Jesus. That is a fact! But while it isn't always easy, having His support makes it more than just bearable - it makes life worth living!

Too often I think people feel that Christians just "don't get it." It can seem like people are telling you to "pray a prayer and it will be Ok." But that is not the message that is found in the Bible. Christ's very followers struggled with belief when they encountered their darkest hour. Even one of

Christ's closest disciples, Peter, denied Him and ran when trial came his way. But Jesus' redemption was bigger than Peter's unbelief and he redeemed him to a life of great purpose (his name actually means "rock" and he later became a powerhouse for Christ in the early Church).

Jesus Christ is bigger than whatever your struggle is, too! He wants to begin the process of redeeming your life to a great purpose. But the keyword in both your story and Peter's story is *process.* While it isn't just a quick prayer and you are now saved, when you surrender your life to Christ and let Him work inside you daily, redemption can continuously happen. You can continuously be perfected in Him. This takes time and patience and trust because it really is a process. The good news is that Christ has all the time in the world – literally! And He will be faithful and true to help you reach your potential.

So there it is: the Truth this entire concept is built on. When we choose to yield, it is Christ that we are yielding to. When we get to the point of surrendering Our Plans and embracing His Reality, it is built on the fact that He is our Lord. In fact, it can only be OK and He can only be our strength if we LET HIM by choosing to enter this beautiful relationship with Him. When we do that, we are throwing our entirety into a union with the God of the universe. The very God who formed the stars and the planets and the mountains and the lakes that we love to look at is waiting to be our *rescuer*. When we let Him be that, He can then start to help us realize the plans and realities we could never fabricate on our own. It is then that we will really start to get results!

Questions:

1) If you know Christ as Savior, in what ways can His redemption continually be bigger than your unbelief?

2) When all is said and done, your response to Christ's offer of salvation will be all that matters. Do you choose to trust and believe Him? Have you surrendered your life to Him?

YIELD

GET RESULTS

YIELD

__John 15:5__ – I am the vine; you are the branches. If you abide in me and I in you, you will bear much fruit; apart from me you can do nothing.

I was reading this recently and it felt like the very first time I had ever seen it. This is one of those verses you hear so many times growing up in church that you kind of forget it actually means anything. At least, that is what had happened for me. But then I recently found myself reading through John from start to finish and a word jumped off the page and rocked me to my core! The word was *ABIDE*.

I used to read this chapter and get caught up in the fruit part. After all, there are vines and branches and harvest and so naturally I looked to the fruit. But what leapt off the page was HOW WE CAN GET THE FRUIT. The fruit and harvest will come in our life only when we choose to *abide* in Him. The nearer we draw to Jesus, the more fruit we will see in our lives. And Jesus tells us in the same chapter that God receives glory when we are bearing fruit! So without drawing near to Christ, we are robbing ourselves of fruit and robbing God of the glory He desires and more importantly deserves! It almost seems too simple.

So how on this earth do we abide? I don't mean that as an expression like Grandma used to say. Really, how do we *abide* while on this earth? Well, Jesus Christ tells us in John 15 that as we draw near to Him, we see an increase in fruit in our lives. We draw nearer to Jesus by spending time in His Word. We draw nearer to Him by spending time in prayer and seeking His will for our lives. We draw nearer to Jesus when we shower Him with worship for Who He is and what He has done!

This can be really hard to live out. I mentioned in Chapter 2 how I am weighing lots of options and feeling the call of ministry on my life. That was 1 month ago when I wrote that and I thought for sure that some answers were right around the corner. So it felt kind of exciting and easy to share at the time. One month is not a very long time, but what has become hard for me and my family is that we feel like we have more questions instead of those highly coveted answers. I don't know about you, but it is easier for me to have faith when I am waiting on an answer or two.

It is much more difficult to remain in faith when the answers don't come but the questions keep piling up!

And so this is why we must ABIDE! I have found myself clinging to Jesus and reading His Word more in the last month than I have in a very long time. I have reminded myself on many occasions that I need to be in deep prayer over these things. I have felt the gut check to really OFFER myself in worship and not just rely on my natural musical gifts to lead songs for other people. It can sound sad and superficial to write it out like that, but it's honest and true. His grace is pushing me through this season and growing me into a new, more perfected version of myself. He wants to do the same for you when you encounter potential changes in your life! But we need to let Him work these things out in His time. A good friend of mine recently shared it with me this way. She is currently in between college and the endless options known as "being a grown up." Just like you and me, she would love some answers! But in her quiet time with God, He led her in this way:

I was reading, "Be still and know that I am God" from Psalm 46:10 this morning. I then sat in silence and this is what I heard:

YIELD

"It's okay that you don't know the plan right now. You're getting to know Me in a new way. And until you know Me in this way, you wouldn't understand the plan even if I told you."

And I replied, "You are the strength and the joy of my heart. I can rely on You."

What a beautiful invitation and what a pure, humble response! Could there be a better way to wait than in growing our relationship with Him? Definitely not! I believe that this invitation is open to you and me as well. God desires to know and to be fully known. Whatever phase of life you find yourself in, take some time to rest in Him and to grow your depth of knowing Him. He is a person with a heart and He desires relationship with you greatly!

While that example is a fairly happy and exciting way to approach abiding in Him, allow me to show you the opposite type of example. Here is a very personal story on what it also can look like to abide:

May 8th, 2015 is a day that will not ever be forgotten. It was two days before Mother's Day and my wife and I had an appointment scheduled to hear our second child's heartbeat. Just 7 weeks before, we had celebrated a positive result on a pregnancy test and looked forward to sharing the news with our families, friends and our social media world on Mother's Day, May 10th. We would have been around 11 weeks pregnant when the news was shared.

The night before our appointment, Erin began to experience some bleeding. This had happened when she was pregnant with our firstborn, Anderson so we just prayed off the fear and believed all would be ok in the morning. Unfortunately, this time was different and it wasn't Ok in the morning. Things got worse throughout the night and a 6 AM call to our midwife confirmed our greatest fear: our baby was in heaven and we would not be hearing a heartbeat or sharing any happy news on Mother's Day. We were (and still are) devastated.

That Mother's Day was an exercise in patience, self-control, love and really just total trust in our Heavenly Father that we could make it through. We made sure to enjoy our beautiful, healthy 14-month-old son Anderson and not just wallow in pity. It wasn't easy, but God's grace got us through. And so here is what this story has to do with abiding in Him:

YIELD

Erin and I could have easily taken a few steps backward in our marriage through this whole ordeal. I'm sure some couples that face this pain do draw apart. It is unbelievably hard to go through! We were hurt, confused and certainly felt ill equipped to deal with such heartbreak. But instead of separating, we just held on to each other even tighter than we ever had before. We drew closer, prayed more, loved more and believed more than we ever really had to before. And God showed us what it really looks like to *abide.*

We learned that "to abide" is to put your well-being and safety in the care of another. It is to lay down ones own abilities to protect themselves and entrust that responsibility to someone else. I'm not drawing that definition from any dictionary or web search. I am sharing it from a real life experience that is still very fresh. For Erin and I, we chose to let Jesus and each other be the comfort that was needed to get through that season. Jesus was my rock and He gave Erin the strength that I needed to see to get through it. And for Erin, Jesus was her rock but He gave me the words and comfort that Erin needed to get through it. It is who He is and it is what He does when we choose to let Him be our protector and our supply. When we choose to *abide.*

That was the hardest time we ever had to go through. But just like Christ's invitation to my friend to "get to know Him better" through her season of waiting, we chose to do the same so that we could have a greater understanding on the other side of this struggle. Whether it's a life plan or the life of your child, lean in hard to Jesus so that you have the help you need in the good and bad times! It will absolutely change your life!

In John 15:7, Jesus tells us that when we surrender our lives over to Him and let Him shine through in the day-to-day, we can be confident that He hears and cares about our requests. He does not promise to make every wish come true, but He does promise to help *perfect* our desires and bring them to pass in a more God-glorifying state than we ever could have intended or created on our own. This is the kind of fruit that I want my life to bring forward!

Just as He directs our steps and makes sure that His purpose stands, when we abide in Him we can be sure that His fruit will be evident in our life – and those around us will be blessed because of it! This is when God begins to receive the glory He deserves and when we begin to experience the true freedom He designed for us.

Questions:

1)   What times in your life have you really felt that you knew what it was to *abide?*

2)   When has God perfected you through a time of waiting or seeking or abiding? Do you need to let Him now?

3)   How can we invite the Father to perfect our desires?

LIVE FREE

YIELD

Galatians 5:13 - It is absolutely clear that God has called you to a free life. Just make sure that you don't use this freedom as an excuse to do whatever you want to do and destroy your freedom. Rather, use your freedom to serve one another in love; that's how freedom grows. (MSG)

Freedom is such a great gift! In our American culture, we celebrate our national freedom several different times a year. It is certainly a part of life that we tend to take for granted because it is literally all we have ever known. But two things stand out to me when I read Galatians 5. First, freedom is not America's idea. It was God's design originally. And second, freedom in Christ actually has a very different meaning than where our American minds tend to go when we hear the word.

So what is the difference between our freedom as citizens of the USA and the freedom we can experience as citizens of His Kingdom? I think it can all be summed up in one word: *depth.*

YIELD

To be born into this great nation and wake up everyday with no fear of persecution or torture or captivity is absolutely one of the greatest blessings I have known in my life. I'm sure I do not even remotely grasp how *deep* of a blessing it really is. I have heard countless stories, and I'm sure you have too, of people visiting other countries and returning to the USA with a greater appreciation and understanding of how good we really do live here. So I am not trying to belittle our great nation at all. But if you can join me and be a just a little bit objective about it, I think you will see that this great natural freedom *pales in comparison* to the freedom that is available to us in Christ Jesus. His supernatural freedom is hard to understand and equally hard to articulate. But I'm going to try:

In chapter 4, I shared with you that in spite of all that this messy world has brought into your life and against your life, Jesus Christ made THE way. He bought you back. He wanted relationship with you and me so badly that He put all of His glory aside to prove it. With His life. And because of His complete work that has created this bridge and looks past all of our downfalls, we are FREE from what haunts us. When we are made new in Christ, we literally have no debt to pay for our wrongdoings because He already took care of it. If that is not freeing, I'm not sure what is! In Galatians 5, Paul is explaining this very same thing but he adds a warning. Don't be so confident in this freedom that you think you have a license to sin. Do not "serve yourself" but look outside of you and "serve one another." Christ gave up everything to provide us with this freedom, now it is our role to respond in love and help His plan for true freedom to grow!

In all honesty, we in America should heed this warning the most. It is so easy in this great country to find opportunities, make money, grow businesses and enjoy recreation. We have no shortage of options and anyone in our country making over $34,000 per year is in the wealthiest 1% in the entire world[1]. We truly are blessed beyond our understanding. And so in knowing that, we need to double down on our resolve to serve one another! We need to up our game so that we don't get swept away into the sea of "self-serving."

It can be so tempting to become comfortable with the blessings that we experience in this country. But as I heard in a great message just the other day, when Christ ascended to heaven He left us with the Holy Spirit or "Comforter." And as the pastor I was listening to shared, the Holy Spirit cannot comfort us unless we are allowing ourselves to become *uncomfortable* for God's glory. Serving others is not a natural desire that we are born with. Ask or observe my toddler, Anderson! But it is what Christ did for us and in turn it is what He has called us to do. This means that when we see things we don't like in another person, we aren't to judge or condemn them. We are to come alongside them in love and try to help them. Christ did a lot of ministry over dinner. I prefer to grab a coffee with people and see how I might be able to help or guide them. Whatever the method is for you, just know that love and patience is the Godly response. Anger or resentment is always your old, sinful self working to keep you comfortable and sabotage God's plan for redemption!

When we abandon our pursuit of personal comfort and use our faith to believe that God will support us in serving others, we grow in ways we could never imagine. We are literally being His instruments of grace and love in a world that needs both so badly. It is true freedom like we have never known! Any of the times that I have chosen to lay down my personal agenda and allow God to use me for His will to be done, I have come away more blessed and joyous than I ever could have imagined! He wants to do the same in your life if you will yield your personal will to Him and love others as He directs you! It is freedom at its best!

Just think of the scope of the freedom God wants us to experience. He so greatly desires our freedom that He has given us the option of being free of *Himself* if we so choose! When He gave mankind free will He gave us the choice between life and death. Unfortunately, we have chosen death more often than life, but in Christ we can now experience the original plan in its restored state: freedom from all sin and shame. Life everlasting with the God who loves us and created us!

Christ's freedom is a deep, cleansing release from all of the wrong we have ever done. It is the offer of a supernatural ability to look past the wrong that has been done to us – and to live free from it all. It actually is *infinitely deep* and could be explored for eternity! When you know Christ as your Savior, it will be explored for eternity! Don't take this lightly; embrace the offer that stands before you. It really will set you FREE.

Questions:

1) How has growing up in America positively affected your understanding of freedom? In what ways has it negatively impacted your view?

2) Why has God chosen to give us free will over all areas of our life including the relationship we have with Him? Does it prove His goodness in a greater way?

3) How beautiful is it to know that Christ offers us a freedom that is *infinitely deep?*

WHAT WORSHIP IS...

YIELD

John 4:23 – *Yet a time is coming and has now come when the true worshipers will worship the Father in Spirit and in truth, for they are the kind of worshipers the Father seeks.*

One of my favorite authors is John Eldredge. I may never really know how much his books and teachings have impacted me. (I have never met him and he did not pay me to write that. I'm just being honest.) But I can tell you there have been times when I have read his books and had truths hit me like a ton of bricks. I remember reading sections of his book *Wild at Heart* early on in my 20's and never having to read those sections again. They were burned into my cerebral cortex, and more importantly, into my spirit.

One of those times was when I read about man's pursuit of Eve's daughters in *Wild at Heart.* When he pointed out that our endless hours of albums and books and poems and literature and artwork were nothing more than *worship*, I felt like I understood worship for the very first time! I had spent my WHOLE LIFE playing music and COUNTLESS HOURS playing in worship bands at churches and youth groups. I really had no context for it though, other than it was what always happened at church or church gatherings. When it was put in the context of *relationship* and *enjoyment,* I felt like it started to actually make some sense.

Isn't it true that when we love something, we celebrate it? I mean, where did weddings and birthdays and parties all come from? They come from our desire to celebrate an occasion or person we are excited about. It is the designed response for our human hearts. Why would we view the worship of our beautiful Savior any differently? We certainly shouldn't, there is PLENTY to celebrate! Freedom from sin and shame. Victory over death. A hope and future in the life that is to come. It is overwhelming!

Unfortunately, we have really cheapened worship. And not exactly on purpose. We have just *served ourselves* and sought freedom in all the wrong places. So we have lost the context of what God originally designed. When you hear your favorite romantic ballad that puts you in just the right mood to text your wife; or you hear that one song from that one summer when you were seeing that one guy or girl, something *moves* inside of you. Your emotions are triggered and your spirit moves. This goes way beyond adolescence or teenage hormones. I know grown men in their 30's who still chase that musical high by performing in bar after bar after bar every night. Music is much deeper than 4 chords and good rhythm. It brings our spirits to life!

It is because of this that Christ desires our worship! He desires our spirits brought to life in celebration of Him and what He has done. His ultimate sacrifice and offer of life is an invitation for us to respond in *loving adoration*. He created us in His image as creative beings because He desires our offerings to Him. Much like (but also much deeper than) the albums that got you through your college finals, worship is the "album" that helps you get through life's ups and downs! It keeps you centered on Him so you don't get too focused on you. He's got you covered, now praise Him for it!

To quote Eldredge, *"Worship is the act of the abandoned heart loving its God. What counts is the posture of the soul involved, the open heart pouring forth its love toward God and communing with Him."* Does that sound like Sunday morning at your church? I am the Worship Pastor at my church and I can honestly say a lot of the times, "No." After a week out in the world, it can be difficult for people to just hand over an "abandoned heart" and "posture their soul" correctly. Even so, it's a real gut check!

Worship is a lifestyle. The Message translation of John 4:23 says "It's who you are and the way you live that count before God." That in and of itself is a freeing statement! When we live surrendered to His authority as who He has designed us to be, He is pleased. He is glorified. He is worshipped – by our surrendered lives! The second half of that verse in the same translation says "...worship must engage your spirit in the pursuit of truth." Amen! That is precisely what we are doing when we allow our spirits to be engaged by the latest Top 100 song and think dreamily of days and significant others gone by. We are looking for truth where it cannot be found, but we are allowing our spirit to be engaged while we do it. God desires that we let our spirit engage but that we pursue Truth where it can only be found – in His Son and our Savior, Christ Jesus. When we allow this to happen, we will truly know and experience great worship! And He deserves nothing less. Our relationship with Him deserves nothing less!

Questions:

1) Do you believe Eldredge's analogy of worship and beauty to be accurate or a bit of a stretch?
2) In what ways can we worship God with our lives each and everyday?
3) How can we use worship to engage our spirit and pursue His Truth?

YIELD

ALL THINGS NEW

YIELD

Revelation 21:5 - *He who was seated on the throne said, "I am making all things new." Then he said, "Write this down, for these words are trustworthy and true."*

Trustworthy and true. That could be it's own book right there. In fact, my favorite name for Jesus is found just a couple of pages over in Revelation 19 – *Faithful and True.* Yes. He really is both of those things! We have proven to be everything but faithful. We have struggled to ever appear true. And yet there is our Jesus. He is everything we could never be and He is more. And so we can't be surprised to find out just 2 chapters later in Revelation 21 that His words and promises are both *trustworthy and true.* It is who He is and it is what He does!

Christ promises that He will make all things new. And in church circles, we repeat that oftentimes because it is encouraging. But when we really dig into it, I think we will find it to be more. I think it is absolutely *life giving!*

YIELD

I have spent a decade trying to figure out how I am at all qualified to be an adult. I can honestly say, I wasn't exactly ready for it at age 21 when I moved out on my own. But my birthday present was the first month's rent paid in full and so I had 30 days to get month 2 lined up. It did not go well and I flailed around like a hyperactive child at swimming lessons for at least the first year (or maybe 3). But in the midst of all the craziness, I had good people around me and I held on for dear life as they helped me to get things under control. I still feel like that hyperactive child from time to time, but I find refuge in knowing there is a God above who has everything under control – in this life now and in the life to come.

While we are here growing our faith and becoming perfected in our walk with God, there are endless truths to be found in His Word for help (I have offered 8 in this book). And the beautiful thing about TRUTH is that it comes from one place – God. So whenever we encounter truth, it always flows back to Him. The Buddhist monk might say something true, but the originator of that truth was not Buddha or the monk. He just said something that God set in motion and therefore it is a truth. We can't let someone's partial accuracy give him or her total credibility. Only God and His Word possess total accuracy and total credibility.

He tells us in this verse from Revelation 21 that not only has he created a way for our free life right now, but He will make everything new in the life to come! All the pain and hurt and tears that we have known will be wiped away and all will become new. It is His promise. And it is trustworthy and true.

If I could live this past decade over again, there are definitely things I would do differently. There are prayers I wish I'd prayed, songs I wish I had written down, and people I wish I hadn't hurt. But in those missteps I have developed an understanding that goes far beyond cause and effect. I have come to know what hurt feels like, I have come to see what regret truly is and I have come to love what redemption brings! It is because of these very real lessons, I hold on to this promise from Revelation 21 and it is why I present it to you as I close out this book. Whatever life has brought your way, there is hope for the future. Believing and trusting in that can give you great comfort in the here and now. No matter how far you have come in the process of growth with Christ, this is still a fallen world and hurt will still happen. But He has promised that a day is coming when all the pain will be wiped away.

When God tells us that He will make "all things new," He speaks of a redemption that brings death to life. He is promising to remove

YIELD

pain that goes as deep as one could ever know. He is showing us once again the scope of His love, His purpose and His control. It is a place where we can lay our burdens down and allow Him to shower us with the peace that passes all human understanding. We honestly cannot comprehend how we will feel no hurt because once you have lived a good bit of life, hurt feels like a constant companion in some ways. But God possesses the ability to create a universe out of nothing and He possesses the ability to take all of your pain and turn it into nothing! He will, because He is trustworthy and He is true! It's who He is and it's what He does. All you have to do is YIELD...

Questions:

1)   How has God shown Himself to be trustworthy and true in your life?
2)   What things does He want to make new in your life? What things do you need Him to make new in your life?
3)   If He chose to do all of that on the other side of eternity, would that be enough for you to completely yield to Him now?

YIELD

Conclusion:

On June 12th, 2015* I sat down at my computer to construct a set list for the next week's worship service at Conduit Ministries in Jamestown, NY. An ad for a self-publishing company (left un-named because they aren't paying me to mention them here) rolled across my screen and I clicked it. I've always wanted to write. I've never known where to start. I saw the nominal price to self-publish a book and I decided I would give it a shot.

Much like the time when God helped a dozen songs flow out of my songwriting partner and I in about 3 weeks, I started writing the outline for this book and had it completed in about 30 minutes. I knew the verses that rang in my head almost daily because the lessons they teach have gotten me to where I am today. I pray that they help you as

YIELD

they continuously help me. I pray that you come to know the true freedom that is found in a life completely yielded to God your Father through Christ your Savior. He is a good, good Father and His purpose is greater than we will ever understand on this side of eternity. Surrender your plan, trust His purpose, abide in Him and pour out your heart in worship. Let Him show you true freedom as you dare to get uncomfortable in His name. He will make all things new!

(June 12th was my Nana Hansen's 86th birthday. I forgot to call her, but I have dedicated this book to her and my Papa. I hope she will forgive me.)

Notes:

Chapter 1: Your Plan

1. God blessed them and said to them, "Be fruitful and increase in number; fill the earth and subdue it. Rule over the fish in the sea and the birds in the sky and over every living creature that moves on the ground."   *-Genesis 1:28*

2. "Start children off on the way they should go, and even when they are old they will not turn from it."   *-Prov. 22:6a*

Chapter 3: It's OK!

1. "Why, you do not even know what will happen tomorrow. What is your life? You are a mist that appears for a little while and then vanishes."   *-James 4:14*

2. *Reuter's Poll, July 1 2013* – "Poll Finds 80 Percent of Workers in Their 20's Want to Change Careers"

Chapter 6: Live Free!

1."The Haves and The Have-Nots" by World Bank Economist Branko Milanovic

YIELD

Acknowledgements

I would like to thank a host of authors who have inspired me, challenged me and helped me grow to places I never could have imagined. I never actually intended to "be a writer" but the things that these folks have indirectly pointed out to me have led to a place that needed to be spilled out on paper. So thank you! This list includes, but is not limited to:

John, Stasi and Sam Eldredge; Chris Vitarelli; Mark Batterson; Dave Ramsey; John C. Maxwell; Jon Acuff; Eugene Peterson; Jefferson Bethke; Og Mandino; Wm. Paul Young and many more!

The greatest of thanks goes out to Jon McCray for designing all of the YIELD cover art! You are one cool cat and I appreciate your patience and excellence with this project.

In the interest of anonymous donations and also not forgetting anyone, I would like to include a blanket THANK YOU to all those who contributed to my Crowd-funding campaign. You helped make a dream become reality and for that I am eternally grateful. I love and appreciate you all!

YIELD

Thank you to Chris Vitarelli, my Youth Pastor, for writing the Foreword and also for sharing your wisdom and encouragement with the project. You encouraged me to write, you gave me feedback during the process and you and Jody sowed seeds 15 years ago that still influence me today. Thank you!!

Lastly, it would be a huge error if I did not mention my Pastors who have aided me, challenged me and guided me through these last 3 very unplanned years in my life. Ben, Corey and Colby, THANK YOU SO MUCH for your patience, love and *constant yielding* to Christ.

YIELD

———————————

Made in the USA
San Bernardino, CA
20 September 2015